How to make a Card

Paul Humphrey

Photography by Chris Fairclough

W
FRANKLIN WATTS
LONDON•SYDNEY

First published in 2006 by
Franklin Watts
338 Euston Road
London NW1 3BH

Franklin Watts Australia
Hachette Children's Books
Level 17/207 Kent Street
Sydney NSW 2000

© 2006 Franklin Watts

ISBN: 0 7496 6606 4 (hbk)
ISBN: 0 7496 6856 3 (pbk)

Dewey classification number: 745.594'1

A CIP catalogue record for this book is available
from the British Library.

Planning and production by Discovery Books Limited
Editor: Rachel Tisdale
Designer: Ian Winton
Photography: Chris Fairclough
Series advisors: Diana Bentley MA and Dee Reid MA,
Fellows of Oxford Brookes University

The author, packager and publisher would like to thank the following
people for their participation in this book: Lucas Tisdale; Auriel and Ottilie
Austin-Baker.

Printed in China

Contents

What you need

Do you like dragons?
Here's how to make
a dragon card.

These are the things you will need:

An old envelope

Some stiff, coloured card

Some stiff, white card

A pencil

PVA glue

Safety scissors

Colouring pens

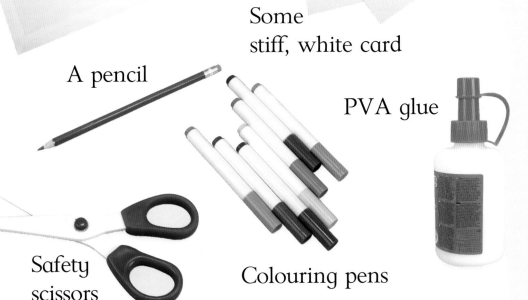

Cutting out the snout

First, draw this shape on the envelope corner. Make it about 10cm along each side.

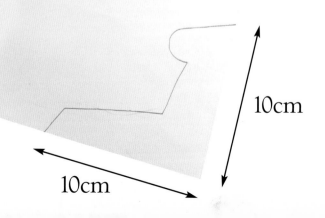

10cm

10cm

Cut out
the shape.

This will be the
snout of the
dragon.

Colouring the snout

Draw on some nostrils
and oval shapes.

Then colour in the
top of the snout.

You can colour in the mouth, too.

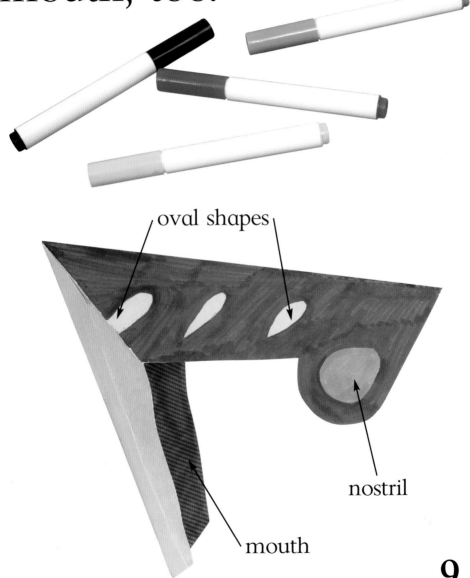

oval shapes

nostril

mouth

Drawing the dragon

Fold the piece of stiff card in half.

Flatten down the fold.

Draw a dragon's face across the inside of the card.

You could add a tail, too.

Colouring the dragon

Next, use the pens to colour in your dragon.

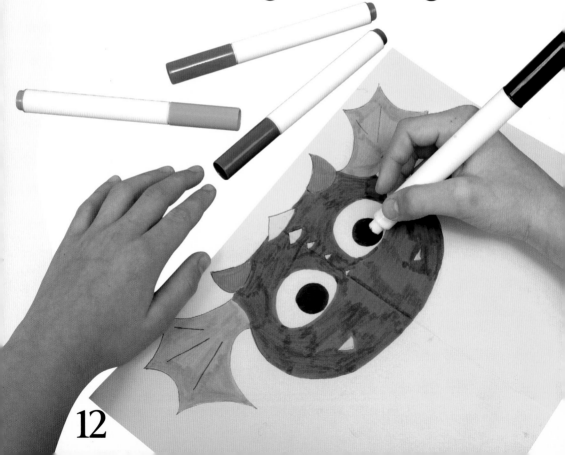

Gluing the snout

Glue the sides of the bottom part of the snout across the inside of the fold.

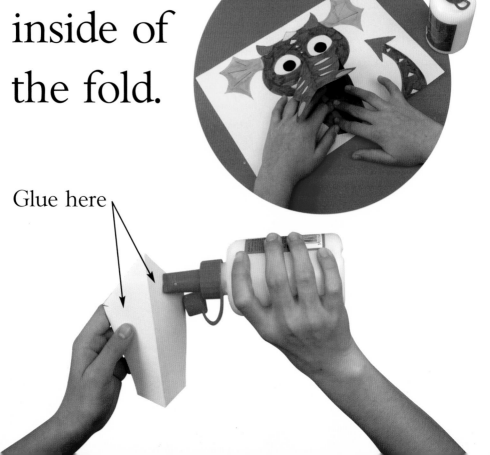

Glue here

Now, close up the card
firmly and leave the
glue to dry.

Opening up the card

Open up
the card.

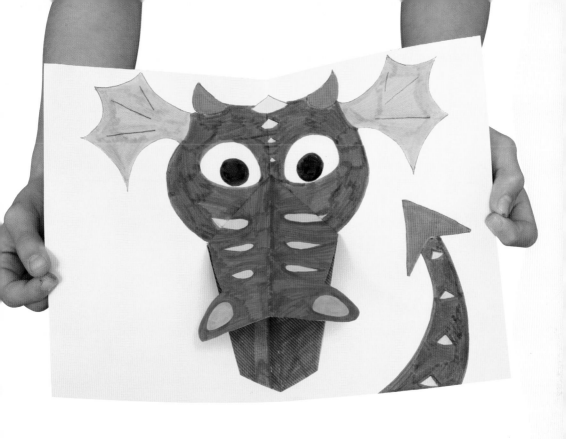

The dragon's snout
moves, too.

Adding the tongue

Cut out a forked tongue.

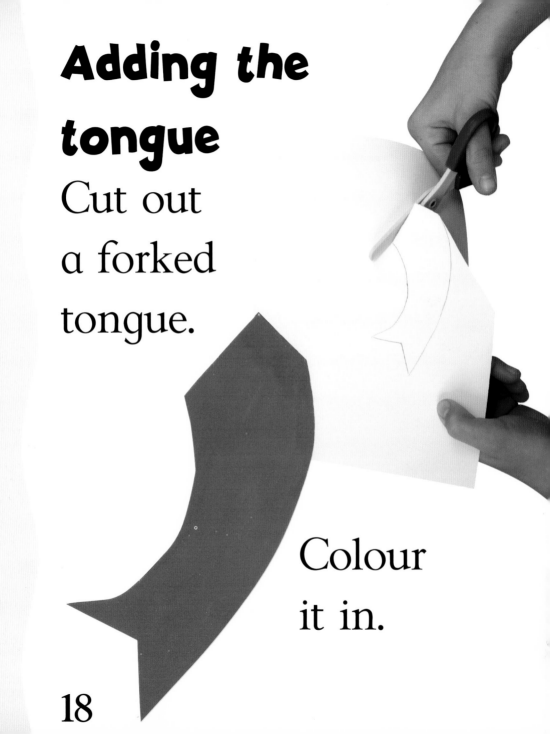

Colour it in.

18

Glue the tongue into the dragon's mouth.

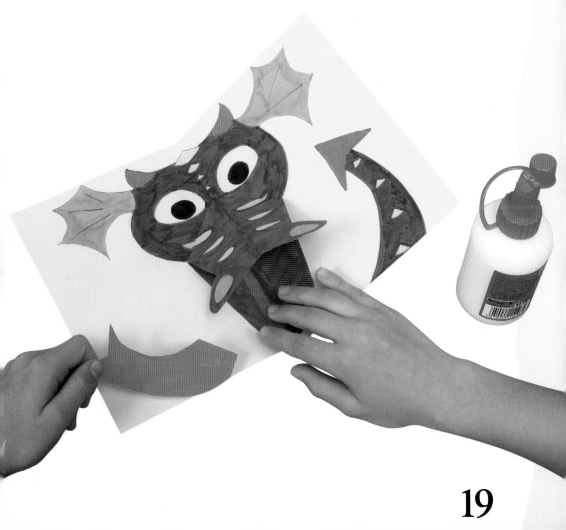

Finishing the card

Now decorate the front of the card.

You could draw a
hidden dragon.

Sending your card

Finally, you can write in your card and send it to a friend.

Steps

Can you remember all of the steps to make your card?

1. Make the snout.

2. Colour in the snout.

3. Fold the card.

4. Draw the dragon.

5. Colour in the dragon.

6. Glue on the snout.

7. Glue on the tongue.

8. Colour in the front of the card.

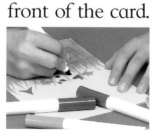

9. Send your card to a friend.